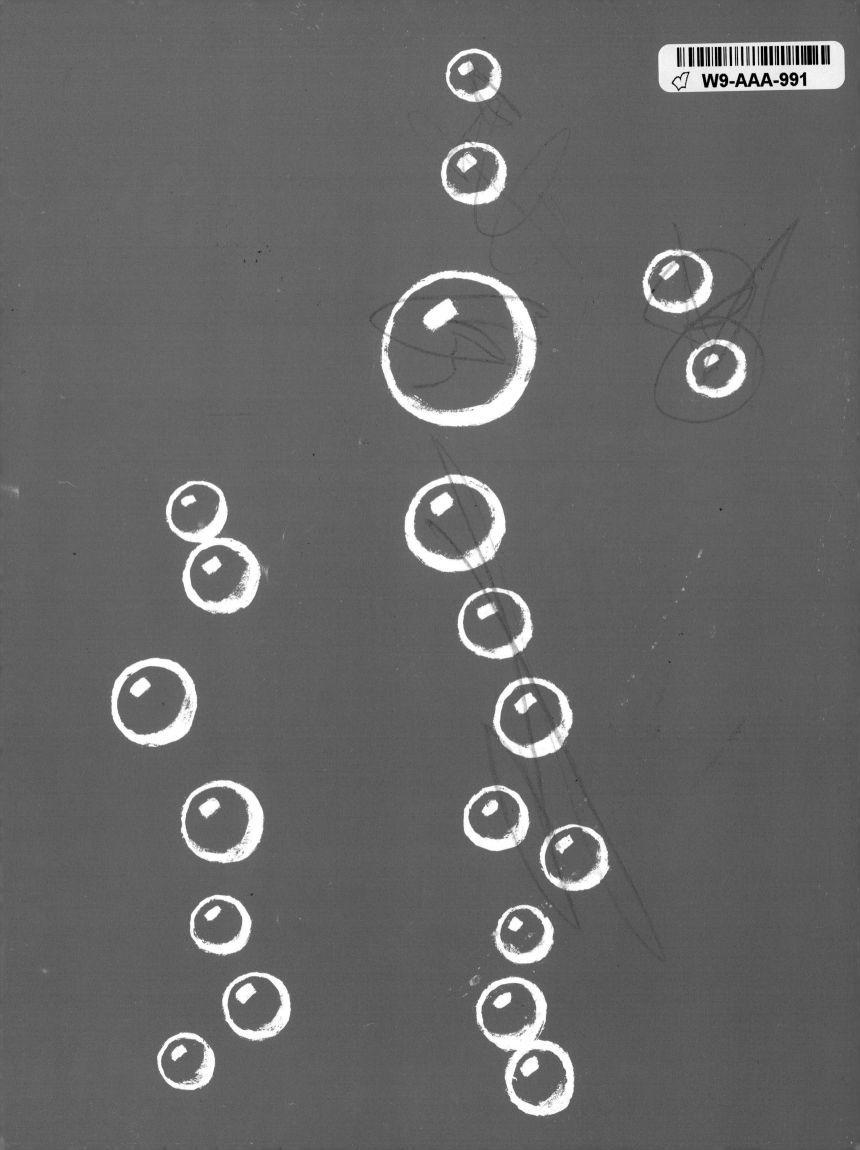

Happy 2nd Birthday Stephen

Lots of Love, XOXO Uncle Norm & Aunt Kath

To Nicholas & Jonah
G.A.

Extra big thanks to Mandy & Jemima
love from David

Other books by Giles Andreae
and David Wojtowycz

Rumble in the Jungle
The Lion Who Wanted To Love

First published in the United States 1998 by Little Tiger Press
N16 W23390 Stoneridge Drive, Waukesha, WI 53188
Originally published in Great Britain 1998 by Orchard Books, London
Text copyright © Giles Andreae 1998
Illustrations copyright © David Wojtowycz 1998
All rights reserved
Library of Congress Cataloging-in-Publication Data
Andreae, Giles. 1966–
Commotion in the ocean / Giles Andreae ; illustrated by David Wojtowycz. p. cm.
Summary : A collection of poems about the many creatures living beneath the sea,
including the crab, dolphin, and angel fish.
1. Marine animals–Juvenile poetry. 2. Children's poetry, English.
[1. Marine animals–Poetry. 2. English poetry.] I. Wojtowycz, David, ill. II. Title.
PR6051.N44C66 1998 821' .914—dc21 98-15772 CIP AC
ISBN 1-888444-39-8 Printed in Belgium First American Edition
1 3 5 7 9 10 8 6 4 2

Commotion in the Ocean

Giles Andreae

Illustrated by

David Wojtowycz

Little Tiger Press

Commotion in the Ocean

There's a curious commotion
At the bottom of the ocean.
I think we ought to go and take a look.

You'll find every sort of creature
That lives beneath the sea
Swimming through the pages of this book.

There are dolphins, whales, and penguins,
There are jellyfish and sharks,
There's the turtle and the big white polar bear.

But can you see behind the wrecks
And in between the rocks?
Let's take a look and find who's hiding there. . . .

Crab

The crab likes walking sideways
And I think the reason why
Is to make himself look sneaky
And pretend that he's a spy.

Turtles

We crawl up the beach from the water
To bury our eggs on dry land.
We lay a whole batch,
And then when they hatch,
They scamper about in the sand.

pitter patter

pitter patter

squeak
squeak

click click

Dolphins

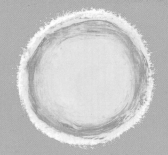

The wonderful thing about dolphins
Is hearing them trying to speak.
It's not "How do you do?"
As I'd say to you.
It's more of a "Click-whistle-squeak!"

whistle

click

Angelfish

Hello, I'm the angelfish, darling,
The prettiest thing in the sea,
What a shame there are no other creatures
As gorgeous and lovely as me!

jiggle jiggle

jiggle

Jellyfish

The jellyfish just loves to jiggle
Which other fish think is quite dumb.
She knows that it's not all that useful
But jiggling's lots of good fun.

Shark

I swim with a grin up to greet you,
See how my jaws open wide.
Why don't you come a bit closer?
Please, take a good look inside. . . .

Swordfish

I love to chase after small fishes,
It keeps me from getting too bored.
And then when I start feeling hungry,
I skewer a few on my sword.

*tickle
tickle*

Octopus

Having eight arms can be useful,
You may think it looks a bit funny,
But it helps me to hold all my children
And tickle each one on the tummy.

tee
hee!

bzzz

bzzz

Stingray

At the bottom of the ocean
The stingray flaps his wings.
But don't you get too close to him,
His tail really stings!

Lobster

Never shake hands with a lobster.

It isn't a wise thing to do.

With a clippety-clap

And a snippety-snap,

He would snip all your fingers in two.

Snippety snap

Clippety clap

Deep Sea

Miles below the surface
Where the water's dark and deep,
Live the most amazing creatures
That you could ever meet.

There are fish of all descriptions,
Of every shape and size.
Some have giant pointy teeth
And great big bulging eyes.

Some of them can walk around
And balance on their fins.
But the strangest fish of all
Have glowing whiskers on their chins!

Blue Whale

There's no other beast on the planet
As big as the giant blue whale.
He measures a massive one hundred feet long
From his head to the tip of his tail.

Walruses

Our bodies are covered with blubber
And our tusks are incredibly long.
We're grumpy and proud
And we bellow out loud
To show that we're mighty and strong.

Uuurggh

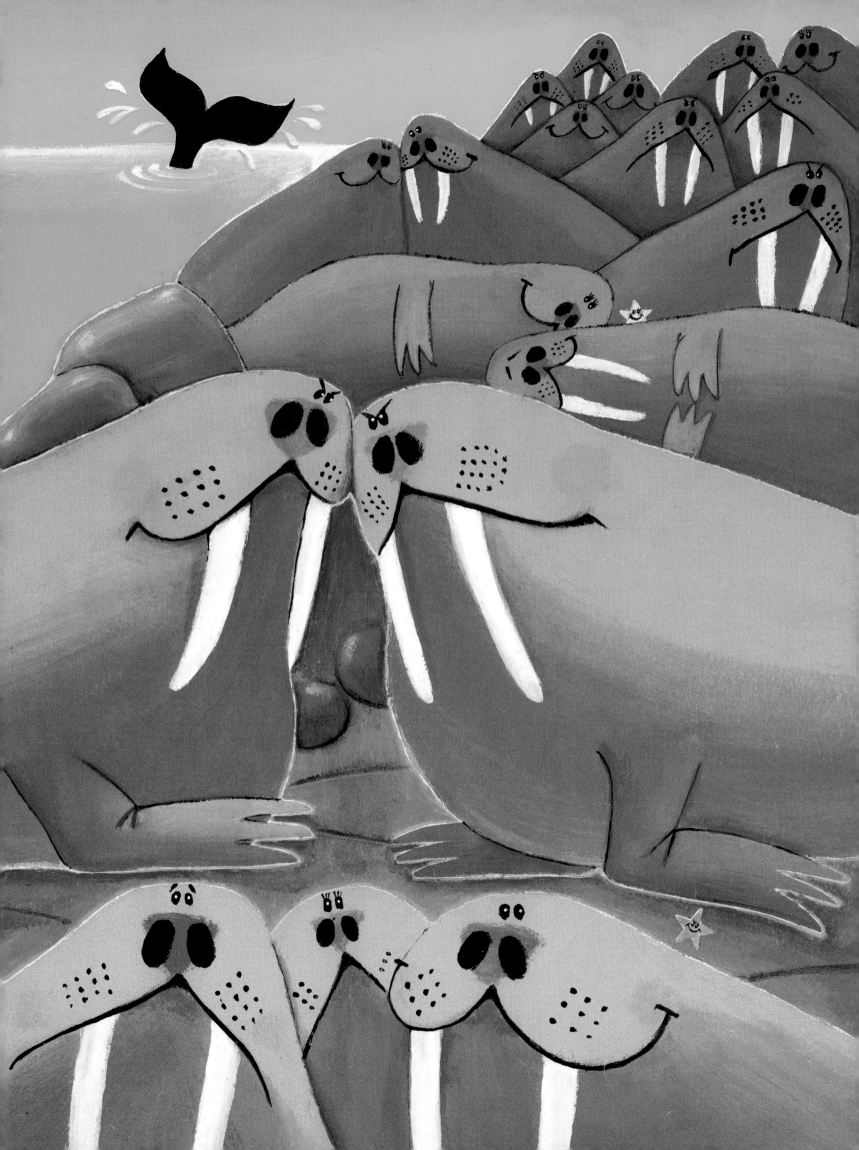

Penguins

Wheeee!

splish

splash

splosh

We waddle around on our icebergs,
Which makes our feet slither and slide.
And when we get close to the water,
We leap with a splash off the side.

Polar Bears

Deep out in the Arctic
The mommy polar bear
Snuggles up with all her children
Since it's very cold out there.

What a lot of creatures
We have seen beneath the sea,
What a lot of funny things they do.

Some of them might lick their lips
And eat you in one bite,
And some might want to swim around with you.

The dolphin's very friendly
And the lobster's very fierce,
But the shark is the most dangerous by far.

Can you name the other friends
We've made along the way?
See if you can tell me who they are.

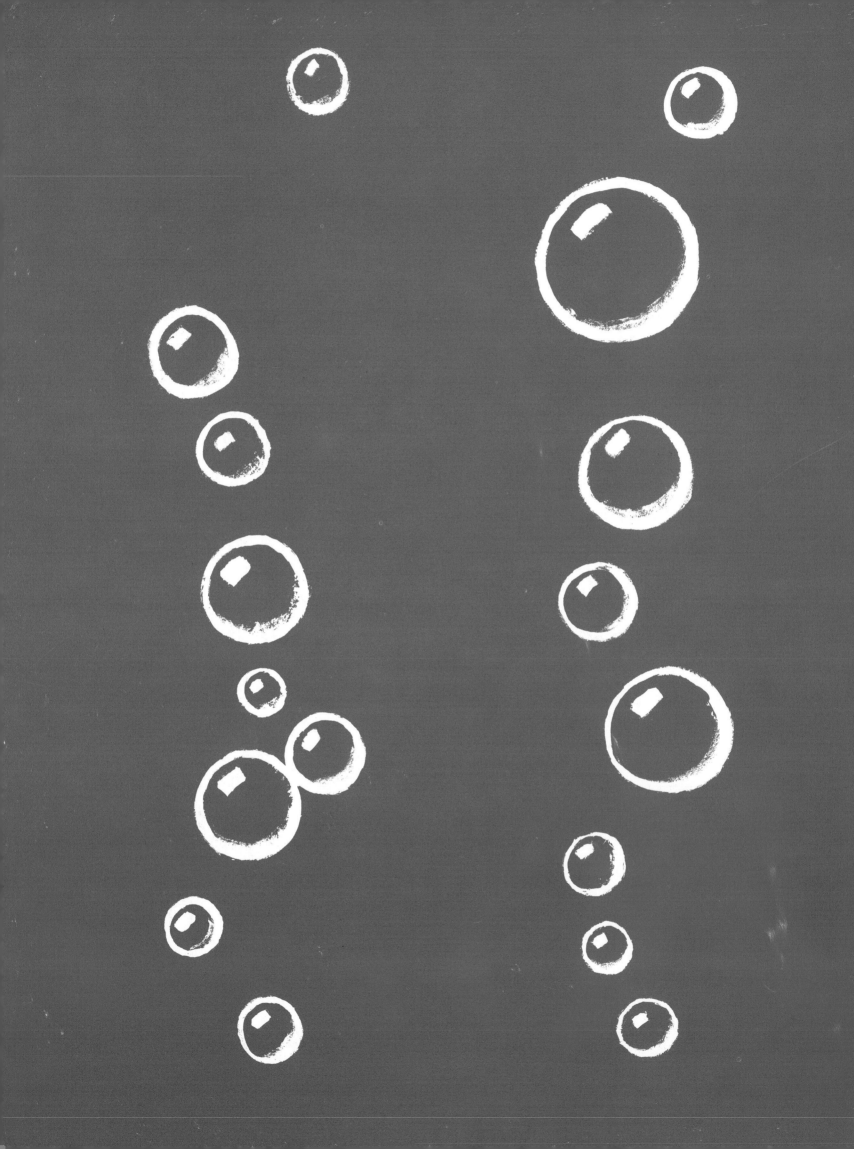